Barry Peckham's NEW FOREST

TEXT BY
BARRY MILES

HALSGROVE

First published in 2001 by Halsgrove
Images © 2001 Barry Peckham
Text © 2001 Barry Miles

British Library Cataloguing-in-Publication Data
A CIP record for this title is available from the British Library

ISBN 1 84114 128 3

HALSGROVE
PUBLISHING, MEDIA AND DISTRIBUTION

Halsgrove House
Lower Moor Way
Tiverton, Devon EX16 6SS
Tel: 01884 243242
Fax: 01884 243325
email sales@halsgrove.com
website www.halsgrove.com

Printed and bound in Italy by Centro Grafico Ambrosiano, Milan

Contents

BARRY PECKHAM

This book is dedicated to my daughters Rachel, Rosalind and Leah.
I would like to thank my wife Sarah for all her help and encouragement.

BARRY MILES

May I thank my wife Jacky and my daughters, Katie and Alice, for all
their patience and co-operation throughout this project.

✑ Introduction ✑

Barry Peckham R.O.I S.E.A

In the south-western corner of Hampshire lies an area of outstanding natural beauty known as the New Forest. Bounded by the Solent to the south, it is an area rich in wildlife with its varied terrain attracting many thousands of visitors each year who marvel at its beauty.

It is also the home of artist Barry Peckham whose oils and watercolours of the area have received international recognition.

Barry is one of the few artists past or present to capture successfully on canvas the very essence of what makes the Forest so special; not only for the thousands who regularly visit, but most importantly for those who live there and know it, as Barry does so intimately.

Whether it be ponies grazing in evening sun on the heaths, or deer lit by morning rays shining through a canopy of summer woodland trees, his observations of light and colour make each painting he produces a true work of art and something to cherish for this and future generations.

EARLY YEARS

He was born a stone's throw from where he now lives, at Ashurst in 1945, in a wooden bungalow and as a boy played in the Forest which backed onto his home. Without the distractions of television, his evenings were spent painting and drawing while any other free time he had was spent playing in his 'other' garden, the New Forest. It was during these early years that his love for the Forest was born, along with the inspiration to try to capture on paper the sights and events he experienced while out on the open heaths or in the secluded woods.

Cholderton Bungalow, Ashurst, where Barry Peckham was born and lived until sixteen-years-old.

After leaving school at fifteen he became an apprentice lathe turner at the Hants and Dorset Bus Company engineering works at Shirley in Southampton where he stayed for six years. During this time Barry started to take an interest in photography and seriously considered it as an alternative career before deciding that his future lay in a different direction.

DEVELOPMENT OF AN ARTIST

It was not until some years later, however, after a casual remark from a friend who was considering starting painting that his interest in art was rekindled. He began studying the works of other leading artists both past and present and visited many galleries up and down the country, some of which were later to hang his paintings.

He was particularly influenced by the small reproduction sketch-books of John Constable who seemed to express in paint and pencil exactly what Barry felt about the landscape although, of course, Constable found his inspiration around his home of East Bergholt in Suffolk. It was Constable who so aptly said: 'But I should paint my own places best, for I associate my own careless boyhood to all that lies on the banks of the Stour.' This is typical of so many artists and certainly applies to Barry whose happy childhood spent in and around the Forest is so gloriously portrayed in his paintings of his own locality.

It is that place association I am sure that drives and inspires many people to paint, and, fortunately for artists, woos members of the public to buy.

THE SIXTIES AND SEVENTIES

During the mid 1960s Barry travelled all over the world, increasing his visual vocabulary and having his eyes opened to the wonders of such places as America, Morocco, Greece and Norway. But his love of the Forest never waned and he was always glad to get back on his home turf after these long excursions abroad. On his return he decided to join the Totton Art Society where he was able to exhibit his paintings, seeking advice and inspiration from some of the Society's more senior and experienced members.

Success soon followed with interest shown from local galleries, important commission work and glowing praise in the local press. By the mid 1970s his confidence was riding high, prompting him to really put his talents to the test by submitting three oil paintings to the Royal Institute of Oil Painters exhibition at the Mall Galleries in London. All three were hung and for the first time Barry felt that he might, at some point in the future, just be able to make a living out of the hobby he had grown to love.

In 1975 he married Georgina Babey and moved to Langley in the Waterside area of Hampshire, once again on the doorstep of his beloved New Forest. He was now painting at every opportunity and had discovered the joy of working directly from nature, carrying his easel and equipment wherever he went.

Although successful in London and nearer to home, Barry still felt the need to improve. In 1976 he took the decision to further his artistic education by enrolling at Southampton College of Art to

An etching by Barry Peckham, *Woodlands*.

study life drawing and etching on a part-time course. He felt these added skills were crucial to his development as an artist, enabling him to take on subjects he would have otherwise found too demanding.

In 1979 Barry and Georgina moved to Woodlands and shortly afterwards started a picture framing business in Totton. This new venture had the added bonus of providing them with a steady income but more importantly enabled Barry to continue to develop his artistic talents when things were quiet in the shop. At home Georgina divided her time between caring for their newly born first child Rachel, and handling the business accounts.

This year also saw him having work hung for the first time at the Royal Academy in London, enhancing his reputation even further.

THE SUCCESS CONTINUES

The 1980s saw more important changes in the Peckham household with their second child Rosalind being born in 1981 and the continuing rise in Barry's popularity as an artist. In 1985 a major commission was undertaken at the request of the Royal Marines in Poole to paint the Special Boat Squadron preparing for combat on Green Island during the Falklands War. Another major commission followed featuring Her Majesty Queen Elizabeth greeting the Royal Marine Officers and their wives in Poole. Both these important works now hang in the officers' mess at Royal Marine Headquarters, Hamworthy.

The following years saw continued artistic achievements while on the domestic front Barry's third daughter Leah was born in 1985. It was in this year that he also became a member of the prestigious Society of Equestrian Artists. Although he was producing some excellent paintings, taking their subject matter from all over the country, it was pictures of his native New Forest that were receiving the greatest praise and admiration as more and more galleries clamoured to handle his work.

Breaking Cover. Commissioned by Royal Marines, Poole, to commemorate
their activities during the Falklands War.

The Queen's Visit, commissioned by the Royal Marines to record H.M. Queen Elizabeth II's visit to the R.M. Headquarters at Poole in 1985.

Following a divorce from Georgina, he was married in 1998 to Sarah and two years later in 2000 achieved one of the finest accolades bestowed on any artist when elected a full member of the Royal Institute of Oil Painters. This honour allows him to exhibit up to six pieces of work each year at the Mall Galleries in London.

Despite all the major successes in Barry's career, the New Forest will always remain his favourite area for painting. The thrill of working directly from nature, able to respond to the ever changing effects of light and weather, with animals roaming freely on the landscape, will provide Barry with an infinite supply of subjects for many years to come.

So whether you are visiting the New Forest or fortunate enough to be one of its residents, be thankful that were it not for the skill and vision of artists such as Barry Peckham, those wondrous views and happy memories would quickly fade. It is a testament to the artist that through his paintings those memories will never be forgotten.

~ Painting Methods ~

OILS

Barry tends to have three separate ways of working in oils and, although not unique in these approaches, the finished paintings do show a remarkable understanding of his medium thus enabling his distinctive atmospheric paintings of the area to really strike a chord with the viewer.

SMALL OIL PAINTINGS

When painting smaller pictures Barry takes all his essential painting equipment with him and sets out to complete the work in one sitting, trying to adapt to any changes in light as he paints.

His palette consists of a range of transparent and opaque colours reflecting the type of subject he intends to paint. The support he uses is either stretched cotton canvas or canvas board, primed with an acrylic primer. He then applies a neutral acrylic wash over the whole canvas which greatly reduces the glare from bright sunlight reflected from the surface. This wash also establishes a useful middle tone that helps in the early and later stages of the work.

The subject is loosely drawn in with paint diluted with white spirit, the sky area applied quickly in a broad manner. Other areas such as shadows and broader darker areas are vigorously scrubbed in using a mixture of transparent colours.

In the final stages of the painting, parts of these areas are over-painted, while others are left uncovered. The painting steadily progresses by adding more and more colour, while all the time the paint on the surface of the canvas is being blended and modified to give shape and form to the subject. Finally, towards the end of the session, a few touches of detail are added which are often vital in determining whether the painting is a success or a failure.

After the paint has completely dried, retouching varnish is applied to the work which can then be framed and made available for exhibition.

In terms of colours, Barry tends to use the following:

Titanium White
Lemon Yellow
Cadmium Yellow (mid)
Yellow Ochre
Raw Sienna
Viridian
Alizarin Crimson
Cadmium Red
Burnt Sienna
Ultramarine Blue
Turquoise Blue
Mineral Violet

LARGE OIL PAINTINGS

For his larger works of more than 20 x 24ins Barry tends to draw a detailed study on location, returning to the studio where he squares the drawing up and copies it onto his canvas, adding a transparent acrylic wash to seal it. He then returns to the same location with all his paints and materials and works over a period of days, sometimes weeks, making sure the light and time of day are all consistent with the mood and atmosphere he wishes to portray.

He prefers to stand while painting and uses a lightweight easel which allows him the freedom to stand back and view the subject and his canvas. This enables him to make any changes before the work becomes too involved and developed. Barry's methods of painting are very much the same as for his smaller oils.

STUDIO WORK

Barry's third way of working differs not in his painting methods or technique but more in his approach to the subject. After arriving at a pre-planned location Barry does a number of sketches and takes some reference photographs of his subject. Then he returns to his studio to transfer it all into an accurate drawing on canvas. Instead of returning to the scene as he would normally do, he relies on the information he has gathered from his colour sketches and photographs to complete the painting entirely in his studio. He generally remains seated while working indoors and often paints commissions by this more controlled way of painting.

Barry Peckham's studio at Ashurst.

WATERCOLOUR

As any artist knows, the characteristics of watercolour are very different from those of oils and, as Barry would be the first to agree, is a much more difficult medium to control. However he is equally proficient in both media and admits he enjoys the freedom, spontaneity and unpredictability that watercolour brings.

Inspired by many of the early pioneers of watercolour such as Cotman, De Wint, Turner and Constable, his fascination with skies and open landscapes is expertly portrayed in his Forest subjects, and watercolour by its very nature and name is an ideal medium for him.

Most of his watercolour paintings are somewhat smaller than his oils as larger scale works done in this medium are likely to be far more prone to disaster and somehow do not have the same intimacy as his smaller works.

Barry tends to use the heavier weights of watercolour paper (200–300lb) as he finds these tend not to buckle and has in recent years turned to Bockingford as his preferred surface for working. This paper has a NOT (slightly textured) surface that easily enables an artist to over-paint and allows some beautiful effects to occur when the wet-in-wet technique is applied. Lifting colour from the paper's surface is also easier than some of the other more expensive makes available. Barry prefers to use quality artist colours from tubes rather than pans and uses sable and synthetic brushes from size 0-15.

He articulates clearly the main differences in his working methods with regard to oil and watercolour. 'With watercolour I tend to flood the paper with a unifying wash, progressively adding stronger washes as the paper dries, while constantly assessing tone and colour values as I paint. Sometimes I lift colour with a damp brush from the paper's surface. The timing, unlike oil, is critical and working into a wash too early or late can have disastrous consequences on the picture with hours of painting time wasted and the whole thing ending up in the bin. The problem with watercolours is that once a mistake has been made it is very difficult to correct and tinkering around with it will only make matters far worse.

'When I intend painting complicated subjects such as street scenes or maritime subjects, I firstly do a detailed drawing directly onto my paper from life. And then, working from light to dark, I paint the larger masses earlier on with the larger brushes, proceeding to add the finer accents and details in the later stages of the work with the smaller brushes.

'For subjects requiring a broader treatment I would merely put in a few brief guidelines and continue painting in much the same way as before.'

PHOTOGRAPHY

Although it might seem strange to include a section about photography in a book on painting, this 'art form' is used by many of today's contemporary artists. Barry finds that photographing the scene, before weather or lighting conditions look set to deteriorate, is better than having to give up on the painting altogether and allows him to at least finish the work in his studio.

There are certain pitfalls, however. One of these is that film cannot always handle the extreme contrasts of light and shade as well as the human eye can and tends to block anything in strong shadow as a black mass. Secondly the camera tends to distort objects, especially buildings, and also includes far too much detail. Thirdly

the illusion of depth in a painting is vitally important for the work to be successful and rarely does the photograph emphasise this fact enough.

'I find that providing I appreciate the limitations of photography and don't fall into the trap of copying, then my camera is a great help, especially for gathering reference material for commission work or for my paintings that need to have slightly more detail than I would normally employ.'

Barry Peckham painting Ashley Heath, New Forest.

~ *Views from Admirers* ~

BARRY MILES

Barry Miles was born in Southampton in 1958 and from an early age has always been interested in art. A keen painter himself, his love of the English landscape has always been his main passion with East Anglia, Dorset, Cornwall, and Hampshire among his favourite areas of study. In 1999 he wrote a book about the painter and teacher Edward Wesson.

'I visited Barry Peckham at his lovely house tucked away from the hustle and bustle of city life and backing onto his beloved New Forest. It was clear from the minute I started talking to him that this was clearly an artist who was content in his own neck of the woods, as it were, and if instructed to never paint outside the area would find enough inspiration to do so until the end of his days. So I asked him what is it about this place that so moves him and many others to express themselves with words, paints, sculpture and photography?'

"For me as an artist, I find the uncultivated wild aspect of the Forest especially appealing with the freedom to walk in the woods and on the open heaths."
'I asked if he could remember his first serious painting.'
"Well if I remember correctly it was of some Roundheads and Cavaliers fighting."
"Not the sort of subject I was expecting from a landscape artist," I commented.
"Ah. But they were fighting in a wood!"

'So the desire to paint gradually developed but it was after reading a book by John Constable illustrating some of his smaller more intimate studies of the land and sky, that Barry was truly hooked, prompting him to search out books by other past masters including Gainsborough, Cotman, and De Wint. He found many of these artists influenced one another and also styles of painting that followed, a notable example being John Constable's influence on the Impressionists in the mid 1800s. This fascination with the history and development of painting revealed many parallels with his own approach to art, and the pleasure of working directly from nature, as so many of his past painting heroes had done, is still very much a part of Barry's own working practices.

'While those early influences shaped and moulded Barry into the painter he is today, he has continued to fine-tune his observations to the extent that subjects which might be considered mundane are transformed into unique masterpieces by his skill and experience with brush and paint. I asked how he sets about choosing a subject or place for painting.

"I have certain places I know will provide me with painterly subjects and assuming the light is good will continue to give me enough material for many years to come; however, there are times when subjects have the habit of finding me and quite often at the most inopportune moments. I remember on one particular occasion after I had been out painting all day, I was feeling rather tired and not too impressed with what I had accomplished so decided to pack up and head for home. As I turned to walk back to the car, I saw a most marvellous full moon rising from a river mist and felt so inspired that I had to settle down, get all my equipment out again and strive to paint it before the light faded.

"This I managed and finished it off back home in my studio. As I had an exhibition coming up I decided to exhibit both the pictures at a gallery in London. Yes, you've guessed. The picture that sold virtually straight away was the one completed in about twenty minutes while the one that I had spent most of the day painting hung around for ages."'

PETER FROST

Peter has been a friend of Barry's for more than 20 years and has just retired from being chairman of The New Forest Association. A keen conservation-

ist, Peter has recently been appointed a Verderer and has accompanied Barry on his painting trips. He runs his own printing business and has reproduced some of Barry's paintings as limited edition prints and cards.

'It was in the late seventies that my wife and I first became aware of Barry's paintings. We both had young children who attended the Woodlands Play group and Netley Marsh Infants School. In those days we had very little money to spare on anything but the essentials of life, with young children and a house that always needed plenty of attention.

'However, we still managed to build up a small collection of "Peckham's". Whether it be oils, watercolours or etchings, each one represents a different stage in our lives, given either as a birthday present from my wife or perhaps an anniversary gift for both of us. The walls of our house are scattered with such pictures and feature many of the subjects Barry finds so appealing. Beech trees, forest streams, churches and rambling old barns are beautifully portrayed and capture that unique and special atmosphere that make the Forest so unique.

'As the years moved on we became good friends and I have travelled with him on rain soaked mountain passes in Wales, and scrambled up huge granite tors on Dartmoor. But despite the adventures further afield, I still regard him as very much a "Forester", suspicious of strangers but generous, loyal and humorous with his friends.

'Barry's dedication to the outdoors subject is compulsive and essential to his aim of capturing nature in the many lights and weather conditions that make his paintings so exciting. Some of the most beautiful moments in nature can last for just a few seconds, and only someone with the speed, confidence and, most importantly, the experience can capture this.

'I have seen Barry attacking a canvas, with paint flying everywhere, while at other times he just stands and waits either for a cloud to pass by or a shaft of light to illuminate a distant hillside. I have seen him painting in the bitter cold and rain with his canvas tipped forward to keep it dry, determined to get down the essential elements of the scene, while I sat and watched from the warmth of a car.

'I remember once, when we were both out painting at Eyeworth Wood, I happened to notice Barry, who was standing about 50 yards away, kicking leaves up in the air in front of his very large canvas. I wondered whether he had been bitten by an adder or was being attacked by an army of wood ants. He later explained that the sun was drying the leaves out too quickly and they were losing their rich colour, and by turning them over he could paint a little longer.

'I think this is a perfect example of how attuned Barry is to colour. Not only does he see colour, he senses it. So next time you see one of Barry's paintings look at it closely and you might just be able to smell those wet leaves.'

ROBERT PERERA

Robert Perera Fine Art of Lymington is a family business of fine art dealers with over thirty years experience in nineteenth and twentieth century New Forest and Marine Paintings. The gallery regularly exhibits Barry's land and seascape paintings.

'Barry Peckham is proving to be a worthy successor to a notable line of New Forest painters. He seems to have taken the strengths of these artists and used them to build his own style and character. Confident brushstrokes, hazy backgrounds, and powerful skies, combined with his understanding of horse movement and anatomy, are all characteristics of Barry's pictures.

'Most notable among New Forest painters are: John Emms (1841-1912) an animal and sporting artist who painted riding, hunting and dog scenes; Arthur Batt (1846-1911) a Brockenhurst artist who started painting forest and rural views and then moved onto animal studies, especially donkeys; similar in choice of subjects, Frederick Golden Short (1863-1936) a keen painter of woodland, open forest and occasional coastline scenes travelled extensively accross the Forest to capture his subject; and finally Lucy Kemp-Welch (1869-1958) a talented horse painter who preferred the natural horse to the thoroughbred, which is also notable in Barry's landscape scenes.

'Barry frequently visits the gallery, having been out to capture the sunrise in the Forest or off to see the evening sun setting over the Solent. Sketching from life, Barry's extensive palette is well suited to the Forest, its coastline and estuaries. Many equestrian artists paint more portrait-style canvasses but Barry's are complete pictures with subject, background and foreground all given equal care and attention.

'His marine paintings, which include *H.M.S. Warrior entering Portsmouth Harbour* and *The Royal Yacht Britannia and Valsheda at*

Cowes Week, show great understanding of the wind, sea, and sky making him worthy of his exhibits at the Royal Society of Marine Artist. Barry is a painter whose work is constantly evolving, while all the time experimenting and refining his technique. An example of this is his revival of the technique of painting on linen, employed by the "Glasgow Boys" in Scotland in the 1890s. Watercolour is worked into the weave which adds a very distinctive texture to the picture.

'The major part of his work is associated with the New Forest and Solent shore but he seems equally at home painting the big skies of Norfolk, small harbours in Cornwall or mountains in Wales, to name but a few. Full membership of the R.O.I. put him within a group of some of the finest contemporary British artists of the day, while full membership of the Equestrian Society shows recognition of his horse compositions. Terrence Cuneo presented Barry with the Cuneo Medal for equestrian painting, a true accolade from one of the twentieth century's leading oil painters.

'Barry is an important painter of today who will be very much remembered in the future and is already noted in many publications including *Who's Who in Art.* We have sold his paintings to collectors in most continents, some on the quality of work alone, while others just want to take a tiny part of this wonderful area, the New Forest, away with them.'

SALLY MITCHELL

Sally Mitchell has been a dealer in equestrian fine art for a number of years and the author of The Dictionary of British Equestrian Artists *published by the Antique Collectors Club. She publishes the work of some of the finest equestrian artists in the country as limited edition prints and greeting cards.*

'It was the great sensitivity of Barry's paintings that first attracted me to them, along with his remarkable use of light. I first saw his work at the Society of Equestrian Artists. His work was so professional I assumed him to be an artist of considerable importance who probably would not have the time for the likes of me, then a little known publisher.

'I was therefore all the more surprised when meeting him for the first time to find such a modest unassuming man who seems to move contentedly through life with little realisation of just how good he really is. Since that first meeting I have got to know Barry quite well and have purchased several of his paintings myself.

'I have also realised that Barry is a true artist who can sit down in the open countryside and capture the light and atmosphere of the day with a few deft brushstrokes. He is equally capable in pastel, watercolour or oil, and whether painting horses, ships, sea or land he has the same abilities of observation, feel for light, atmosphere, colour and composition that make all his paintings so special. He has the knowledge, or genius, I'm not sure which, to know where to put the few important brushstrokes that make his paintings come alive. He also has the rare ability of knowing when to stop which is of equal importance.

'Whenever I see ponies in the New Forest I will see Barry's pictures and when I look at his pictures I will be back in the Forest.'

∽ *The Paintings* ∾

A comprehensive selection of Barry's work over recent years is shown on the following pages. The paintings are grouped together according to the subjects that are so close to Barry's heart – heathlands, nature and wildlife, woodland, buildings, coastal and marine, and human interest.

Some of the pictures are accompanied by personal comments which help to give a better understanding of Barry's inspiration and approach to that particular subject.

~ *Heathlands* ~

The heathlands of the New Forest cover over 30,000 acres containing the largest and most varied forms of wildlife in southern England. During July and August the heaths are covered with ling and bell heather in vast tracts of pink and purple flowers which, interspersed with the bright yellow flowers of the gorse (known locally as 'furze'), create almost impenetrable protection for birds such as the Dartford Warbler. This fantastic patchwork of changing colours from springtime to late autumn provides Barry with a wealth of painting subjects.

He prefers the northern section of the Forest where he finds the terrain most appealing and can regularly be seen painting on Ashley Heath, Stone Quarry Bottom and Blackgutter Bottom.

It is arresting to consider, that this long steep valley he so often enjoys painting was used by the Dam Busters to practise dropping their 'bouncing bombs' during the Second World War and that one was found just a few years ago in the valley. What a contrast to the peace and tranquility one finds there today.

The area is clearly special to him. 'It's a long wide valley and when you have a partly cloudy sky you get beautiful areas of light and shade up and down the side of the heath, creating the most amazing colours. Sometimes a white pony in the distance might just for a second be caught by the sun, providing just the focal point to a painting you had been searching for.'

When it comes to painting the famous New Forest ponies (such a trademark of his work) there is nothing to beat a little local knowledge and experience of where to find these animals. Barry has many such places where he can return time and time again to paint his marvellous oils.

'The ponies and cattle do have their favourite areas for grazing and congregating and these are known as "shades". When I go to these areas I normally have two or three hours where the animals' movements are minimal which allows me to get the basic composition and drawing done before the group break up and move to higher ground.'

Barry generally works in oils on the heathlands and has worked on canvasses as large as as 40 x 60 inches on these more exposed areas of the Forest.

Summer
oil (28 x 36in)

Longwater
oil (16 x 22in)

Hampton Ridge
oil (10 x 14in)

Millersford Bottom
oil (24 x 40in)

'In the valley below Deadman Hill lies Millersford. On a spring morning with the gorse in flower, ponies wander down to drink from the brook. At this time of year in the valley, the light can often be exceptional. I return here frequently, always finding new subjects to commit to canvas.'

Penn Common
watercolour (11 x 14in)

Ashley Shade
oil (18 x 28in)

Deadman Hill
oil (20 x 28in)

Ditchend Brook
oil (14 x 18in)

Mogshade
oil (16 x 30in)

Ashley Walk
oil (40 x 45in)

'Cloud shadows race along the valley floor creating a changing pattern of light and shade. This valley in former years was the location for the R.A.F. to practise prior to the famous Dam Busters Raid during the Second World War. Thirty years later parts of the "bouncing bomb" were recovered from Ashley Walk, reconstructed and presented to 617 Squadron who had carried out the raid. The presentation took place at R.A.F. Middle Wallop and was attended by the inventor of the bomb, Sir Barnes Wallis and two of the pilots who flew the Lancasters.'

Below Godshill Ridge
oil (12 x 16in)

Crossing the Brook
oil (24 x 30in)

Cockley Hill
oil (12 x 16in)

The Clear Stream
oil (24 x 20in)

Crossing the Ford
oil (22 x 28in)

Hillside Grazing
oil (12 x 18in)

Longwater
oil (18 x 26in)

'A heavy downpour has created a pattern of puddles on the low-lying heath-land. Nearby the infant Beaulieu River drains the water and carries it on its journey to the Solent.'

Rockford Common
oil (16 x 20in)

The Pool
oil (20 x 30in)

Indian Summer
oil   (20 x 12in)

The Clear Brook
oil (30 x 36in)

The Meeting Place
oil (30 x 40in)

Snowfall, Longdown
oil (10 x 14in)

Whitemoor Ridge
oil (14 x 28in)

'Ponies stand on the hillside catching the last warm rays of the sun. Speed is essential when trying to capture an evening sky such as this. The colours change rapidly while all the time the approaching darkness makes it difficult to see the correct mixtures on the palette.'

Ponies Near Godshill
oil (30 x 60in)

~ Nature & Wildlife ~

Although the natural wildlife is of paramount importance to the Forest, it does not play such a major role in Barry's paintings. While ponies and cattle feature frequently, foxes, deer and badgers appear only occasionally. 'This is not because I find them any less appealing but more to do with the fact that they provide a welcome change from the intense concentration of land and seascape painting.

'In fact this closer look at nature can reveal a fascinating source of subject matter and between April 1986 and April 1987 I produced a small sketchbook of nature studies. Once a week I would select a detail and paint it in watercolour, adding the time, date and location. After a full year I had painted 52 such studies covering the four seasons and these have provided me with a valuable source of reference for some of my larger paintings.'

Fox in Waiting
oil (10 x 12in)

'I occasionally encounter wildlife when painting in quiet places. One afternoon, whilst engrossed in a small painting, I heard a sound behind me. Upon turning, I was surprised to see an equally startled fox. He had not noticed me standing quietly until he was just a few yards away. He had caught a small rabbit and was on his way home. Unable to make any sense of what I was doing, he turned and crept off through the bracken.'

Rabbit's Playground
oil (14 x 18in)

Deer, Puckpits Wood
oil (8 x 10in)

Downton Meadows
oil (24 x 30in)

'The rich red of the dock leaves in the foreground contrasts well against the varied greens of the meadow beyond. The geese provide added interest without dominating the scene.'

❧ *Woodland* ❧

The woodland areas of the Forest are almost as extensive as the heathlands and for many people the most popular. Whether it be the romanticism of Norman kings hunting deer, so well recorded in our history books, the escape from the hustle and bustle of busy urban life, or just an appreciation of the wildlife and beauty to be found there, the woodlands have provided inspiration for thousands of walkers, naturalists, artists, writers and photographers throughout their long and varied history.

Composed of ancient and ornamental woodlands, hardwood and coniferous enclosures, this mosaic of different habitats contains a multitude of plant and animal species with oak, beech, Scots pine, ash and birch being the most common tree species. In contrast to the heathland, Barry prefers the autumn and winter months of the woodland areas and finds the enclosed, more intimate, atmosphere a real challenge to capture on canvas.

'I find the colour and structure of the trees far more interesting than in the summer months with the rich siennas and browns of the dead or dying leaves a constant inspiration. Ashurst Wood is probably one of my favourite areas and is only a short distance from where I live so I know it extremely well, at all times of the day, in all seasons and all weathers.

'Because it is so heavily grazed by the ponies one can see the structure of the trees more clearly which helps to simplify the compositions of my paintings.

'Although the arrival of autumn makes the woods visually exciting, this can bring its own problems with the scene constantly changing almost by the minute, leaving little time to complete paintings. During the winter months, however, I can spend more time on my paintings and return to a scene many times, observing the frequent subtle variations of light that occur rather than the rapid change of spring and autumn.'

As to which of the many woodland trees he prefers to paint, Barry says, 'I find beech trees particularly attractive with their interesting shaped trunks and smooth bark often covered in bright green moss on their exposed roots. This provides a nice contrast with the reds yellows and browns of fallen leaves.'

Barry is very aware that he follows a long line of successful New Forest painters and feels part of this strong tradition while endeavouring to make his own statement and mark for for future generations to enjoy.

Ponies in Matley Wood
oil (40 x 60in)

Roman Bridge
watercolour/gouache (7 x 9in)

Autumn
oil (16 x 20in)

Winter Sun, Ashurst Wood
oil (24 x 30in)

Waiting for the Winter Feed
oil (16 x 30in)

'When the grazing becomes scarce during the harsh winter months, many commoners take food out to their animals. The ponies soon learn when it is due to arrive and gather, patiently waiting. These groups of ponies provide excellent opportunities for sketching and supply numerous ideas for paintings as they move around, constantly rearranging themselves.'

Oakley Wood
oil (8 x 10in)

Lucy Hill
oil   (20 x 24in)

'I had noticed this stand of pines when driving past and made a mental note to return to paint them. The ground in front had been cleared, revealing the slender trunks and patchwork of light and dark standing out against a clear blue sky.'

Across the Meadow
oil (24 x 30in)

The White Pony
oil (18 x 28in)

Shatterford Pines
oil (24 x 30in)

Denny Wood, Evening Light
watercolour (7 x 11in)

Ancient Beeches
oil   (7 x 10in)

Winter, Matley Wood
oil (18 x 28in)

Forest Pool, Lyndhurst Hill
oil (7 x 9in)

Beeches, Whiteshoot
oil (8 x 10in)

In the Trees
oil (18 x 36in)

Pigs in Ashurst Wood
oil (16 x 20in)

'In the autumn commoners have the right to turn out pigs into the Forest. This is called Panage or Rights of Mast. The pigs' main diet during this time consists of the newly fallen acorns. The inclusion of the pigs into a landscape adds interest and acts as a reminder that once wild boar roamed these woods.'

The Larch
oil (12 x 10in)

Pony, Emery Down
watercolour (8 x 10in)

Last of the Snow, Matley
oil (12 x 16in)

Bolderwood
oil (16 x 22in)

'Snow transforms a landscape and makes us look at it with a fresh eye. Usually the foreground would be the darker and warmer feature in a landscape scene but in this painting, the reverse is the case.'

Denny Wood
watercolour (11 x 14in)

Mallard Wood
oil (24 x 48in)

Beech, Highland Water
oil (10 x 12in)

Mallard Mead
oil (20 x 24in)

Morning
oil (30 x 40in)

'The subjects I choose to paint are selected for a number of reasons, often depending upon what type of mood I am in. An expansive mood resulted in the painting *Morning*. It was painted at great speed using large brushes whilst I endeavored to capture the myriad of colours produced by the sun on the dew-soaked leaves of the brambles.'

Gritnam Wood
oil (12 x 16in)

Winter Oaks
oil   (20 x 24in)

Dunces Arch
oil (18 x 36in)

'A detailed drawing preceded this painting. This was necessary due to the intricate pattern of branches against the winter sky. The painting was worked on over a number of days when identical weather conditions occurred. The wet leaves reflect the light from the weak sun and produce subtle colour changes.'

Rowbarrow Wood
oil (28 x 36in)

Deerleap
oil (16 x 20in)

'The diversity of the New Forest landscape is of great value to an artist seeking variety. The conifer wood with its tall trees provides welcome shade from the heat of the sun flooding the small clearing. This is a simple subject but is made interesting by the effects of the light.'

79

In the Shadows
oil (16 x 32in)

Storm Damage
watercolour (7 x 10in)

Ashurst Wood
oil (30 x 48in)

The Pine Wood
oil (16 x 20in)

'The impressionistic approach in the painting impressed the judges of the Laing Painting Competition enough for them to use it on their 1992 calendar. I find that the subject itself dictates whether a loose or detailed application is used in a painting. In this case, the patchwork of the sun and shadow breaking the uniformity of the straight trunks suggested a broad treatment.'

83

~ Buildings ~

Although the New Forest does not have anything like the number of buildings as the nearby cities and towns of Lymington, Christchurch, Bournemouth and Southampton, it still hosts some fascinating examples of fine architecture with Bucklers Hard, Beaulieu, and Lyndhurst, all places worth visiting.

It is a combination of the history, along with the shapes and weathering effects on these buildings, that really interests and inspires Barry to portray this type of subject. Cottages, churches and barns all feature heavily in his paintings and in 1994 a highly successful book was published and illustrated by Barry, entitled *Churches of the New Forest*.

'I find the way buildings become integrated into the landscape over a period of maybe hundreds of years of particular interest, and with the addition of ponies or horses into the composition, clearly identify that this is very much New Forest country.'

Lymington Market
oil (12 x 16in)

Beaulieu Mill
watercolour (13 x 10in)

Ashlett Mill
watercolour (11 x 14in)

Pigs at Nomansland
watercolour (6 x 8in)

Smallholding, Longdown
oil (20 x 30in)

'This smallholding lies on the eastern boundary of the Forest. The interesting collection of old buildings is coloured with the subtle tints that only time and weather can produce.'

Robinsbush Farm
oil (14 x 18in)

Boldre Church
watercolour (7 x 11in)

'In a quiet lane, this lovely church dating from the eleventh century has been the subject for several of my paintings. During the eighteenth century the vicar of Boldre, William Gilpin, wrote and illustrated *Remarks On Forest Scenery*, now regarded as a classic work on the New Forest landscape.'

Farm at Sowley
watercolour (7 x 11in)

Donkey by a Barn
watercolour (9 x 7in)

Barn at Cuckoo Hill
watercolour   (11 x 14in)

The Royal Oak, Fritham
oil (16 x 20in)

'The isolation of this public house at the end of a country lane makes it a favourite with local foresters. Many years ago, it acquired the unofficial title of "Parliament of the New Forest", due to the meetings and discussions that took place in the back parlour.'

Newtown Barn
watercolour (11 x 14in)

Lodge Farm
watercolour (8 x 11in)

Lyndhurst
oil (16 x 22in)

'"The capital of the New Forest" is the title that Lyndhurst claims. Before cattle grids were introduced to keep the animals out of the village, scenes like this were commonplace. The church stands high above the houses, making a good focal point. Inside the church is a fresco painted by Lord Leighton and some of the windows were designed by members of the Pre-Raphaelite Brotherhood.'

Bucklers Hard
watercolour (11 x 14in)

The Gate House
watercolour (14 x 22in)

∽ Coastal & Marine ∽

Where the Forest meets the waters of the Solent, between the mouths of the Lymington and Beaulieu Rivers, extensive mud flats and salt marshes are home to an abundance of waders and wildfowl. Barry finds these coastal areas especially interesting and a great number of his most successful paintings have featured Milford on Sea, Keyhaven and the particularly impressive Hurst Castle and lighthouse at the end of a mile-long pebble spit.

'Although this section of the Hampshire coast has not the drama or spectacular cliffs and picturesque harbours of its Dorset neighbour, I do find the place has its own unique atmosphere and one I repeatedly return to. My favourite view is looking across the Solent with the tiny white sails of the yachts picked out against the darker backdrop of the Isle of Wight.'

Further east one can see the unusual sight of New Forest ponies ambling along the beach. 'The changing tide can also provide the artist with many exciting opportunities and under different weather conditions offer an infinite supply of material. In fact, these types of scenes often give a far wider range of atmospheric effects than the more enclosed environment of the woodlands as quite often the sky is hardly visible.'

Regarding the media Barry prefers in trying to capture these elusive lighting effects, he tends to favour watercolours. 'Because these subjects are of water with large expanses of sky above I tend to apply a looser, broader approach and watercolour is the ideal medium for this. The other important fact is that although the seasons do, of course, affect the coast as they do the rest of the landscape, the visual impact is not as noticeable and I find I am able to paint them all year round.'

Calshot Castle
oil (12 x 24in)

The Solent Shore
oil (24 x 36in)

'The character of the Forest's coastal boundary is well illustrated in this paint-ing. Both cattle and ponies roam the shoreline, adding an extra element of interest against the backdrop of the Solent and the Isle of Wight.'

Gilbury Moorings
watercolour (7 x 10in)

The Royal Yacht Britannia, *Cowes Week*
oil (22 x 30in)

'The Solent forms the southern boundary of the New Forest and often features in the paintings I produce along the shoreline. Occasionally I get the opportunity to get to closer grips with the sea as in this painting. During Cowes Week, all types of craft can be seen. Here a J. Class yacht passes across the bows of the anchored Royal Yacht *Britannia*.'

Lymington Harbour
oil (7 x 9in)

Evening Light, Pylewell
watercolour (7 x 9in)

Barge at Bucklers Hard
oil (12 x 24in)

'Arriving at Bucklers Hard I was agreeably surprised to find a barge moored at the water's edge. An opportunity too good to miss, I was soon working at top speed thinking it might be moved at any minute. It was good to see an older vessel that served as a reminder of when Bucklers Hard was a thriving boat-building yard in earlier times.'

Cattle by the Solent
oil (12 x 24in)

Ponies by the Solent
oil (14 x 26in)

Calshot
watercolour (11 x 15in)

The Jetty, Bucklers Hard
watercolour (14 x 22in)

Keyhaven
oil   (12 x 16in)

'The small harbour of Keyhaven is a lively place with fishing boats and a yacht club. The size is part of its charm and I always find new subjects to commit to canvas whenever I return. If an early scheme to bore a tunnel to the Isle of Wight from Keyhaven had gone ahead, the nature of the place would have changed dramatically.'

The Bait Diggers
oil (20 x 24in)

Cottage on the Shore
oil (12 x 16in)

'The receding tide left puddles reflecting the warm light of the winter sunset. As the day ended, the shore became quiet as I added the finishing touches to the painting. Apart from me, only a solitary bait digger remained on the water's edge.'

Mudeford Quay
watercolour (11 x 15in)

Pylewell Marsh
watercolour (7 x 10in)

High Tide at Keyhaven
watercolour (11 x 22in)

The Bait Digger, Keyhaven
oil (9 x 14in)

Gilbury Hard
oil (14 x 18in)

'The contrast of the moored yacht against the silver light on the wet mud attracted me to this scene. The nature of the river is that it is ever changing. The movement of craft and the effects of weather and tide provide endless subjects for painters.'

119

Beachcombers
watercolour (7 x 11in)

Inchmery
oil (8 x 10in)

On the Beaulieu River
watercolour (14 x 20in)

Beaulieu Estuary
oil (12 x 24in)

Shoreline Shade
oil (18 x 24in)

Saltmarsh Grazing
oil (16 x 20in)

Pitts Deep
oil (12 x 24in)

The Lymington Estuary
oil (14 x 28in)

ᴄ Human Interest ᴇ

Of the many human activities that go on in the Forest, those involving the ponies are Barry's main interest. The pony round-ups, stallion inspections and point to point races have all inspired him to produce memorable paintings. His motivation is not just the excitement and action of these events, but an awareness of the stark reality that unless recorded on canvas or photograph, many will be remembered only by words. This he feels would be a tragedy for future generations.

'Some of these scenes could well have been painted by Sir Alfred Munnings a century ago and have changed little in the last few hundred years. One of the events I find most exciting is the pony sale held between April and November at Beaulieu Road Station. This is one of the most important events in the New Forest calendar and attracts many people. I like to wander in and out of the pens sketching the ponies and drawing some of the local characters.

'The New Forest Show is another colourful event in the Forest year which is open to the general public. I particularly like to find a quiet area to sketch and draw, choosing a modest subject that I can then develop into a larger work back in my studio.'

The Pony Sales
oil (24 x 36in)

'The scene depicted here took place in April at the first sales of the year. The painting records events that have probably not changed very much in the last 100 years. It was with this in mind that I wanted to show a slice of Forest life at the end of the twentieth century.'

129

The Sales, Beaulieu Road
oil (36 x 42in)

The Pony Drift
oil (16 x 24in)

Down to the Pound
oil (18 x 28in)

Turf Hill Pound
oil (30 x 40in)

'The pony round-ups, or drifts, take place each year during the late summer and autumn. Once located, ponies are channelled by riders into containing areas where they are penned ready for tail marking, worming or branding. Most are later released back into the Forest. All the activity provides a wealth of material that can later be considered in the studio for potential future paintings.'

133

The Ploughing Match
watercolour (16 x 20in)

Heads in Line
oil (16 x 32in)

'The New Forest Show is an annual event in the Forest. While there is much activity of interest in the main show rings, I often find good subjects for paintings tucked away in quiet corners.'

The Heavies
oil (16 x 20in)

The Charcoal Burners
oil (16 x 22in)

'Charcoal burners would once have been a familiar sight in the Forest but now they are rarely seen. This painting was produced from reference I gathered during the early 1970s when the burners were working in Church Place Inclosure near Ashurst.'

The Morning Ride
watercolour (9 x 12in)

The Commoner
oil (24 x 36in)

Pete Fishing, Royden Wood
oil (16 x 20in)

'Peter is a very good friend of mine. He has recently taken up painting and often accompanies me on painting trips. Peter has filled the post of Chairman of the New Forest Association for seventeen years and has been untiring in his efforts to protect the natural and historic heritage of the New Forest. When time permits, he likes nothing more than to spend a few hours in quiet isolation indulging his passion for fishing.'

Penn Common Pony Roundup
oil (12 x 24in)

The New Forest Point to Point Race on Boxing Day
oil (18 x 28in)

'After the excesses of Christmas Day, I welcome the opportunity of some fresh air and the annual point to point offers a good excuse. The races are divided into several categories and involve a variety of distances. The competitors know where the finish is but the starting point is not revealed until the morning of the race, when they are taken out to it. From there, they have to use not only speed but also their knowledge of the Forest to get to the finishing post first.'

Rosalind, Leah and Rachel
oil (20 x 24in)

Further Reading

Trevor Chamberlain, *Oils* (Anaya Publications Ltd, London, 1993)

Rowland Hilder, *Sketching Country* (The Herbert Press, London, 1991)

Jack Merriott, *Discovering Watercolour* (Pitman, London, 1973)

Edward Wesson, *My Corner of the Field* (Alexander Gallery, Bristol, 1982)

Barry Miles, *Edward Wesson 1910–1983* (Halsgrove, 1999)

Wilfrid Ball & Rev. Telford Varley, *Hampshire* (Adam & Charles Black, London, 1909)

Leonard Richmond, *Landscape Painting Step-by-Step* (Watson Guptill, 1978)

Alfred W. Rich, *Watercolour Painting* (Seely, Service and Co. Limited, 1918)

Adrian Bury, *Watercolour Painting of Today* (The Studio Ltd., London, 1937)

Gordon Beningfield, *Beningfield's English Landscape* (Viking/Penguin Books Ltd., 1985)

Percy V. Bradshaw & Ernest W. Haslehust, *I Wish I Could Paint* (The Studio Publications, London and New York, 1945)

Edward Seago, *A Canvas To Cover* (Collins, 1947)

Caroline Fox, *Stanhope Forbes and the Newlyn School* (David & Charles)

Laura Wortley, *Lucy Kemp-Welch/The Spirit of the Horse* (Antique Collectors Club, 1988)

W. Heaton Cooper, *Mountain Painter* (Frank Peters Publishing, 1984)

Stanley Booth, *Sir Alfred Munnings 1878-1959* (Sotherby Parke Bernet Publications, 1978)

Iain Gale, *Arthur Melville* (Atelier Books)

David Curtis, *A Light Touch/Painting Landscapes in Oils* (David & Charles)

Leslie Worth, *The Practice of Watercolour* (Pitman, 1977)

Charles A. Hall, *British Trees* (A. & C. Black Ltd., 1930)

Adrian Hill, *On the Mastery of Watercolour Painting* (Pitman, 1939)

Aubrey Phillips, *Watercolour Painting with Aubrey Phillips* (Batsford, 1997)